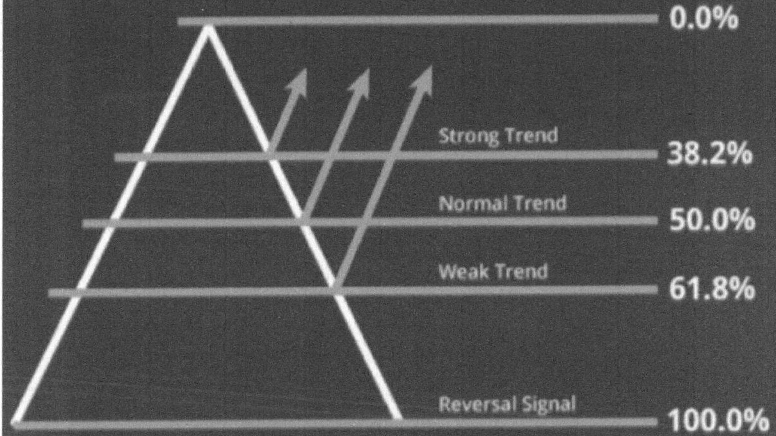

Elliote Wave Theory

Rules, Guidelines, and Basic Structures

By Khalid Madih

Elliote Wave Theory

Khalid Madih

Published by Khalid Madih, 2023.

While every precaution has been taken in the preparation of this book, the publisher assumes no responsibility for errors or omissions, or for damages resulting from the use of the information contained herein.

ELLIOTE WAVE THEORY

First edition. August 7, 2023.

ISBN: 979-8223935957

Written by Khalid Madih.

Also by Khalid Madih

Elliote Wave Theory

Table of Contents

To my loving family, who has been my constant support and inspiration. Your unwavering love and encouragement have been the driving force behind my journey. This achievement is dedicated to each of you. Thank you for always believing in me.

The ideal choice for trading with a higher probability of winning.

By Khalid Madih

In the world of financial markets, traders and investors constantly seek methods to gain an edge, to decipher the elusive patterns of price movements. Among the numerous trading strategies, one approach has stood the test of time, captivating the attention of traders worldwide – the Elliott Wave Theory.

1) Elliott Wave Theory: Modern Theory for 21st Century Market

2) Fibonacci

3) Motive Waves

4) Elliott Waves Personality

5) Corrective Waves

1) Elliott Wave Theory: Modern Theory for 21st Century Market

1.1 What is Elliott Wave Theory?

Elliott Wave Theory is named after Ralph Nelson Elliott (28 July 1871 – 15 January 1948), an American accountant and author. Influenced by the Dow Theory and inspired by observations in nature, Elliott postulated that the stock market's movement could be forecasted by recognizing a repetitive pattern of waves.

By delving deeper into market analysis, Elliott identified distinct characteristics of wave patterns and made precise market predictions based on them. While his work was partially based on the Dow Theory, which also interprets price movement in waves, Elliott uncovered the fractal nature of market behavior. In 1938, he published his groundbreaking theory of market patterns in a book titled "The Wave Principle." Through this work, Elliott provided traders and investors with a new perspective on understanding and predicting market trends through the lens of wave patterns.

1.2 Basic Principle of the 1930's Elliott Wave Theory

In simple terms, the Elliott Wave Theory suggests that market movements follow a specific patterns. When the market is trending, it unfolds in a series of five waves, known as the motive wave. On the other hand, when there's a correction against the trend, it occurs in three waves, called the corrective wave. These waves are labeled numerically (1, 2, 3, 4, 5) for the motive wave and alphabetically (a, b, c) for the corrective wave.

These patterns are observable in both long-term and short-term charts. Moreover, smaller patterns can be found within bigger patterns. In this analogy, Elliott Waves resemble a piece of broccoli – the smaller pieces look like the larger piece when broken off. This information, along with the Fibonacci relationships between the waves, allows traders to anticipate and predict potential trading opportunities with favorable reward-to-risk ratios. By understanding these wave patterns, traders can gain valuable insights into the market's direction and make more informed trading decisions.

1.3 The Five Waves Pattern (Motive and Corrective)

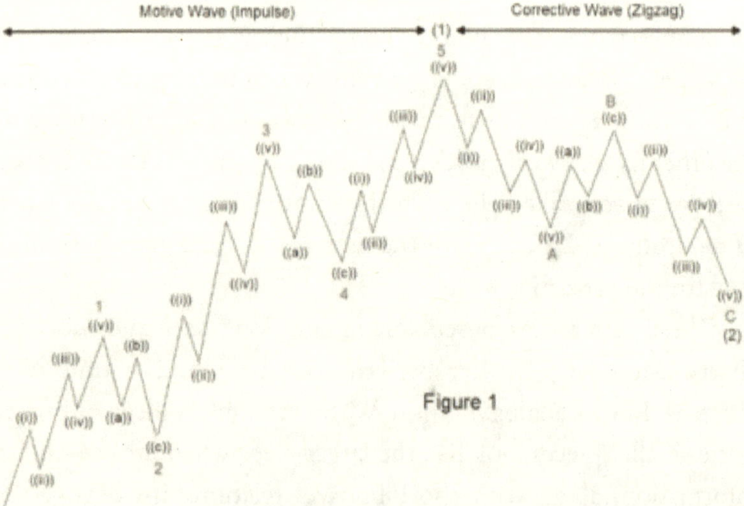

Figure 1

In Elliott's model, market prices exhibit a cyclical pattern, alternating between two phases on all time scales of trend. The first phase is called the impulsive or motive phase, while the second phase is the corrective phase. Impulses consist of five lower-degree waves, alternating between motive and corrective character. Waves 1, 3, and 5 are motive waves, while waves 2 and 4 are smaller retracements of waves 1 and 3.

In Figure 1, we observe wave 1, 3, and 5 as motive waves, each subdivided into 5 smaller degree impulses labeled as ((i)), ((ii)), ((iii)), ((iv)), and ((v)). Conversely, wave 2 and 4 are corrective waves, consisting of 3 smaller degree waves marked as ((a)), ((b)), and ((c)). Together, these 5 waves (1, 2, 3, 4, and 5) form a larger degree motive wave (1).

On the other hand, corrective waves are composed of 3 smaller-degree waves, denoted as ABC. They begin with a five-wave counter-trend impulse (wave A), followed by a retrace (wave B), and conclude with another impulse (wave C). These 3 waves (A, B, and C) constitute a larger degree corrective wave (2).

In a bear market, the dominant trend is downward, resulting in a reversal of the patterns five waves down and three waves up. This repetitive structure of impulse and corrective waves allows traders to identify potential trading opportunities and predict market movements with a greater level of confidence.

Grand Super Cycle :	((I)) (((II)) (((III))((IV))((V)) ((a)) ((b))((c)) ((w)) ((x)) ((y))
Super Cycle	: (I) (II) (III) (IV) (V) (a) (b) (c) (w) (x) (y)
Cycle	: I II III IV V a b c w x y
Primary	: ((1)) ((2)) ((3)) ((4)) ((5)) ((A)) ((B)) ((C)) ((W)) ((X)) ((Y))
Intermediate	: (1) (2) (3) (4) (5) (A) (B) (C) (W) (X) (Y)
Minor	: 1 2 3 4 5 A B C W X Y
Minute	: ((i)) ((ii)) ((iii)) ((iv)) ((v)) ((a)) ((b)) ((c)) ((w)) ((x)) ((y))
Minutte	: (i) (ii) (iii)(iv)(v) (a) (b) (c) (w) (x) (y)
Subminutte	: i ii iii iv v a b c w x y

The Elliott Wave degree is a language used to categorize cycles, enabling analysts to determine the position of a wave within the broader market progression. Elliott recognized nine degrees of waves, ranging from the Grand Super Cycle degree, typically observed in weekly and monthly time frames, to the Subminuette degree, which is identified in hourly time frames. This degree classification scheme is applied to all of EWF's charts, allowing for a comprehensive understanding of wave patterns and trends across various time frames.

1.5 The Rise of Algorithmic / Computer-based Trading

The 21st century has been shaped and characterized by the remarkable advancement of computer technology and the Internet. This progress has led to the proliferation of computer-based and algorithmic trading, giving rise to a new category of traders who rely solely on technical analysis, probabilities, and statistical data, devoid of emotional aspects. These automated systems execute trades at ultra-fast speeds, often within seconds or milliseconds, based on proprietary algorithms.

Undoubtedly, the trading landscape today is vastly different from that of the 1930s when Elliott first developed his wave principle. With such radical changes in the trading environment, legitimate questions arise regarding the applicability of the Elliott Wave Principle in today's markets. It's akin to expecting modern cars to differ significantly from those of the 1930s, leading us to question whether a trading technique developed in the 1930s can still be relevant in today's dynamic trading landscape.

1.6 The New Elliott Wave Principle – What is Changing in Today's Market

The most significant difference between today's market and the one in the 1930s lies in the definition of a trend and counter-trend move. In the modern trading landscape, we encounter four major market classes: the stock market, forex, commodities, and bonds. Originally derived from the observation of the stock market (i.e., Dow Theory), the Elliott Wave Theory was primarily developed with a focus on the stock market. However, certain markets, such as forex, exhibit more of a ranging market behavior.

While 5-wave moves still occur in today's market, our years of observation suggest that 3-wave moves happen more frequently than 5-wave moves. Additionally, the market can exhibit a corrective structure that continues in the same direction, deviating from the traditional 5-wave trend pattern. In other words, the market can trend in a corrective structure, advancing in a sequence of 3 waves, experiencing a pullback, and then resuming the same direction again in a 3-wave corrective move. Therefore, in today's market, trends do not have to adhere strictly to the traditional 5-wave patterns, and trends can unfold in 3 waves as well. It is essential not to force everything into 5 waves when analyzing trends and labeling the chart, as the market's behavior may deviate from traditional Elliott Wave patterns.

2) Fibonacci

2.1 Introduction

Leonardo Fibonacci da Pisa, a thirteenth-century mathematician, is renowned for discovering the Fibonacci sequence. In 1242, he published a paper titled "Liber Abacci," which introduced the decimal system. This groundbreaking work was inspired by a two-year study of the pyramids at Giza. However, Fibonacci's most famous contribution was the Fibonacci Summation series, which played a vital role in the transition of the Old World in the 13th century from Roman numerals (e.g., XXIV = 24) to the Arabic numbering system (24) that we use today. For his exceptional work in mathematics, Fibonacci was honored with the equivalent of today's Nobel Prize. His legacy continues to be celebrated for its profound impact on numerical systems and mathematical understanding.

2.2 Fibonacci Summation Series

One of Leonardo Fibonacci's most popular discoveries is the Fibonacci Summation series. This series begins with 0 and 1 as the first two numbers. Each succeeding number in the series is obtained by adding the previous two numbers, creating a sequence of 0, 1, 1, 2, 3, 5, 8, 13, 21, 34, 55, 89, and so on, continuing to infinity.

The Golden Ratio (1.618) is derived from the Fibonacci series by dividing a Fibonacci number with another previous Fibonacci number in the sequence. For instance, dividing 89 by 55 yields the Golden Ratio, which is approximately 1.618. This intriguing mathematical relationship has fascinated mathematicians, artists, and scientists for centuries due to its occurrence in nature and its aesthetic appeal in various forms of art and architecture.

2.3 Fibonacci Ratio Table

Various Fibonacci ratios can be generated in a table, as shown below, by dividing one Fibonacci number (numerator) by another Fibonacci number (denominator). These ratios, along with several others derived from them, are prevalent in nature and the financial markets. They frequently signal levels of significant resistance and support. These ratios are prominently observed in nature, such as seashell spirals, flower petals, the structure of tree branches, and more. They also manifest in art, geometry, architecture, and music, captivating the imagination and influencing various creative endeavors.

Fibonacci Ratio Table

Numerator

Denominator	1	2	3	5	8	13	21	34	55	89	144
1	1.00000	2.00000	3.00000	5.00000	8.00000	13.00000	21.00000	34.00000	55.00000	89.00000	144.00000
2	0.50000	1.00000	1.50000	2.50000	4.00000	6.50000	10.50000	17.00000	27.50000	44.50000	72.00000
3	0.33333	0.66667	1.00000	1.66667	2.66667	4.33333	7.00000	11.33333	18.33333	29.66667	48.00000
5	0.20000	0.40000	0.60000	1.00000	1.60000	2.60000	4.20000	6.80000	11.00000	17.80000	28.80000
8	0.12500	0.25000	0.37500	0.62500	1.00000	1.62500	2.62500	4.25000	6.87500	11.12500	18.00000
13	0.07692	0.15385	0.23077	0.38462	0.61538	1.00000	1.61538	2.61538	4.23077	6.84615	11.07692
21	0.04762	0.09524	0.14286	0.23810	0.38095	0.61905	1.00000	1.61905	2.61905	4.23810	6.85714
34	0.02941	0.05882	0.08824	0.14706	0.23529	0.38235	0.61765	1.00000	1.61765	2.61765	4.23529
55	0.01818	0.03636	0.05455	0.09091	0.14545	0.23636	0.38182	0.61818	1.00000	1.61818	2.61818
89	0.01124	0.02247	0.03371	0.05618	0.08989	0.14607	0.23596	0.38202	0.61798	1.00000	1.61798
144	0.00694	0.01389	0.02083	0.03472	0.05556	0.09028	0.14583	0.23611	0.38194	0.61806	1.00000

Toward Perfect Ratios

Some of the key Fibonacci ratios can be derived as follows:

- 0.618 is obtained by dividing any Fibonacci number in the sequence by another Fibonacci number that immediately follows it. For example, 8 divided by 13 or 55 divided by 89.

• 0.382 is obtained by dividing any Fibonacci number in the sequence by another Fibonacci number that is found two places to the right in the sequence. For example, 34 divided by 89.

• 1.618 (Golden Ratio) is derived by dividing any Fibonacci number in the sequence by another Fibonacci number that is found one place to the left in the sequence. For example, 89 divided by 55 or 144 divided by 89.

These ratios play a significant role in various aspects of life, including nature, art, architecture, and financial markets. They often indicate key levels of support and resistance and have a profound influence on design and aesthetics due to their inherent harmony and balance.

2.4 Fibonacci Retracement and Extension

Fibonacci Retracement, both in technical analysis and Elliott Wave Theory, refers to a market correction or counter-trend movement that is anticipated to find support or resistance at specific key Fibonacci levels. Traders and analysts use these levels to identify potential reversal points, where the market is expected to turn and resume its primary direction.

On the other hand, Fibonacci Extension pertains to the market moving in alignment with the primary trend towards areas of support or resistance at key Fibonacci levels. Traders utilize Fibonacci Extension levels to measure their target profit when aiming for potential price objectives.

Below is a list of important Fibonacci Retracement and Fibonacci Extension ratios commonly used in the financial market:

Fibonacci Retracement Levels:

- 23.6%
- 38.2%
- 50%
- 61.8%
- 78.6%

Fibonacci Extension Levels:

- 61.8%
- 100%
- 161.8%
- 261.8%
- 423.6%

These Fibonacci ratios serve as essential tools for traders and investors, helping them identify potential entry and exit points while navigating the dynamic movements of the financial markets.

Retracement	• 14.6%(0.146) • 23.6%(0.236) • 38.2%(0.382) • 61.8%(0.618) • 76.4%(0.764) • 85.4%(0.854)
Extension	• 61.8%(0.618) • 100%(1.00) • 123.6%(1.236) • 161.8%(1.618) • 200%(2.00) • 261.8%(2.618) • 323.6%(3.236) • 423.6%(4.236)

2.5 Relation Between Fibonacci and Elliott Wave Theory

Fibonacci Ratios are highly valuable in measuring the target of a wave's movement within an Elliott Wave structure. These ratios establish meaningful relationships between different waves in the Elliott Wave pattern. For example, in an impulse wave:

- Wave 2 typically retraces to 50%, 61.8%, 76.4%, or 85.4% of wave 1.
- Wave 3 typically extends to 161.8% of wave 1.
- Wave 4 typically retraces to 14.6%, 23.6%, or 38.2% of wave 3.
- Wave 5 typically reaches an extension of 1.236% to 1.618% of wave 4, equals wave 1, or reaches 61.8% of the combined length of wave 1 and wave 3.

By understanding these Fibonacci relationships, traders gain valuable insights for determining optimal entry points and profit targets when initiating a trade. The application of Fibonacci Ratios in Elliott Wave analysis enables traders to enhance their trading decisions and seize potential opportunities with greater precision.

3) Motive Waves

In Elliott Wave Theory, the traditional definition of a motive wave is a 5-wave move that aligns with the trend of one larger degree. There are three variations of a 5-wave move considered as a motive wave: Impulse wave, Impulse with extension, and diagonal.

However, EWF (Elliott Wave Forecast) chooses to define motive waves differently. While we agree that motive waves move in the same direction as the trend and that a 5-wave move constitutes a motive wave, we believe that motive waves do not necessarily have to be limited to 5 waves. In today's market, motive waves can unfold in 3 waves as well. Due to this observation, we prefer to refer to it as a motive sequence instead.

By recognizing this broader perspective of motive waves, we adapt our analysis to better align with the current market dynamics, ensuring a comprehensive and accurate understanding of wave patterns and trends.

3.1 Impulse

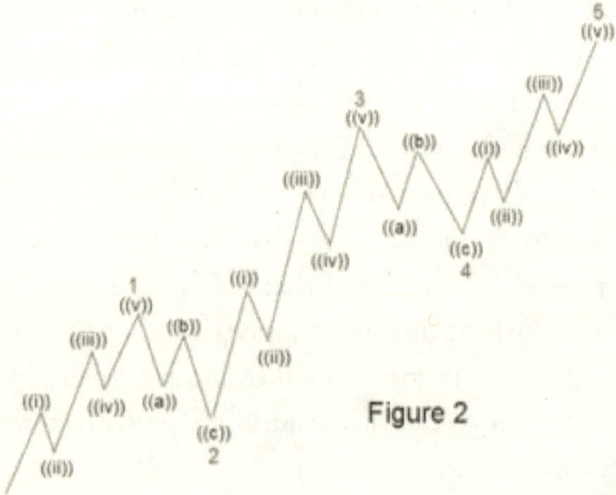

Figure 2

Guidelines for Impulse Waves:

• Impulse waves subdivide into 5 waves. In Figure 2, the impulse move is subdivided as 1, 2, 3, 4, and 5 in minor degree.

• Waves 1, 3, and 5 subdivisions are impulses, represented as ((i)), ((ii)), ((iii)), ((iv)), and ((v)) in minute degree.

• Wave 2 cannot retrace more than the starting point of wave 1.

• Wave 3 should not be the shortest among waves 1, 3, and 5 (the three impulse waves).

• Wave 4 must not overlap with the price territory of wave 1.

• Wave 5 needs to end with momentum divergence.

Fibonacci Ratio Relationship for Impulse Waves:

• Wave 2 typically retraces to 50%, 61.8%, 76.4%, or 85.4% of wave 1.

• Wave 3 generally extends to 161.8%, 200%, 261.8%, or 323.6% of the length between wave 1 and wave 2.

• Wave 4 typically retraces to 14.6%, 23.6%, or 38.2% of the length between wave 3, but it should not exceed 50% of that length.

• There are three different ways to measure wave 5: First, wave 5 is typically an inverse retracement of 123.6% to 161.8% of the length of wave 4. Second, wave 5 can be equal in length to wave 1. Third, wave 5 may extend to 61.8% of the combined length of wave 1 and wave 3.

By adhering to these guidelines and Fibonacci relationships, traders and analysts can effectively identify and interpret impulse waves within the Elliott Wave structure, assisting them in making informed trading decisions.

3.2 Impulse with Extension

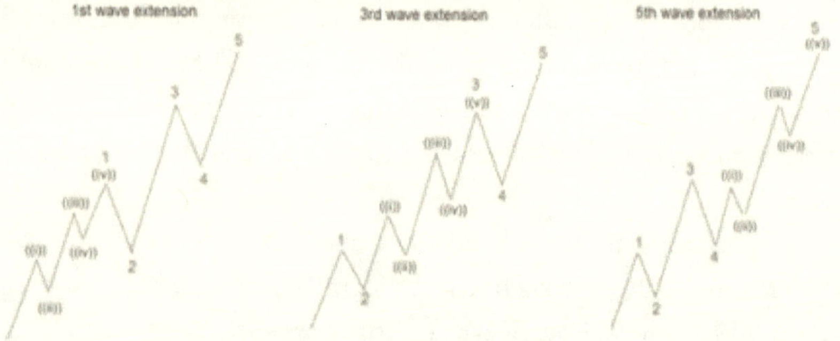

Figure 3

Guidelines for Impulse Waves:

- Impulses often exhibit an extension in one of the motive waves, specifically in wave 1, 3, or 5.
- Extensions represent elongated impulses with exaggerated subdivisions, making them stand out in the wave structure.
- In the stock market and forex market, extensions are frequently observed in the third wave.
- Conversely, the commodities market commonly experiences extensions in the fifth wave.

By recognizing these patterns of extensions within impulse waves, traders and analysts can gain valuable insights into potential price movements and market trends, aiding them in making well-informed trading decisions.

3.3 Leading Diagonal

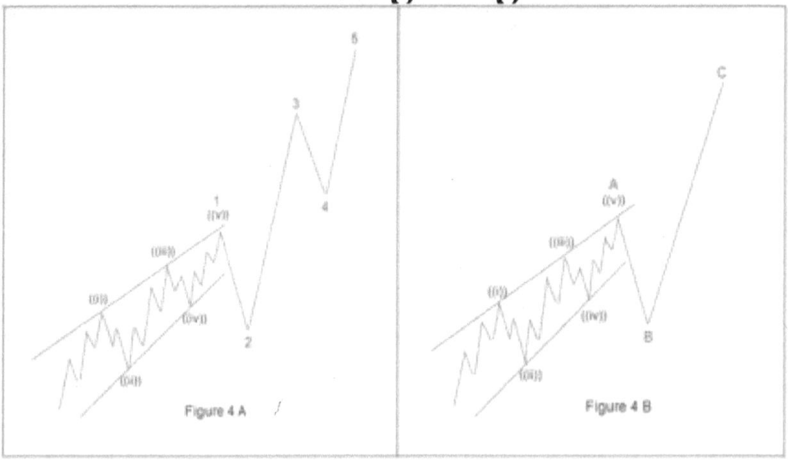

Figure 4 A

Figure 4 B

Guidelines for Leading Diagonals:

- A leading diagonal is a special type of motive wave that can appear as a subdivision of wave 1 within an impulse or as a subdivision of wave A within a zigzag correction.
- In Figure 4A, the leading diagonal is a subdivision of wave 1 in an impulse. In Figure 4B, the leading diagonal is a subdivision of wave A in a zigzag correction.
- Leading diagonals are usually characterized by having overlapping wave 1 and 4, and they often form a wedge shape. However, it's important to note that the overlap between wave 1 and 4 is not a strict condition; it may or may not happen.
- The subdivision of a leading diagonal can follow either a 5-3-5-3-5 or a 3-3-3-3-3 pattern. The examples provided above illustrate a leading diagonal with a 5-3-5-3-5 subdivision.

By recognizing the features of leading diagonals, traders and analysts can enhance their understanding of this unique wave pattern within the Elliott Wave structure, allowing for more accurate analysis and forecasting in the financial markets.

3.4 Ending Diagonal

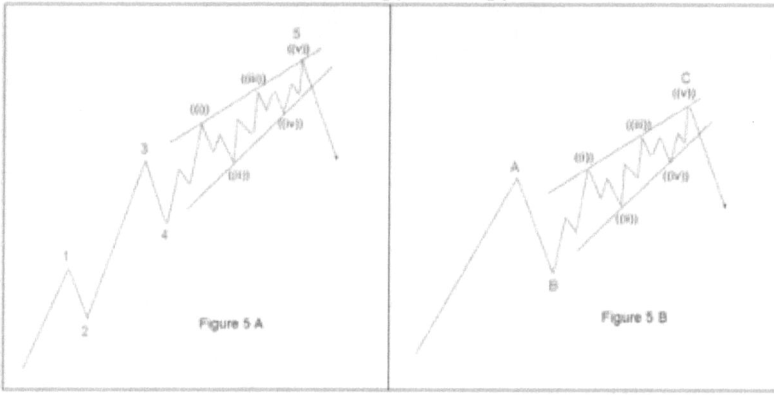

Guidelines for Ending Diagonals:

• An ending diagonal is a special type of motive wave that can appear as a subdivision of wave 5 within an impulse or as a subdivision of wave C within a zigzag correction.

• In Figure 5A, the ending diagonal is a subdivision of wave 5 in an impulse. In Figure 5B, the ending diagonal is a subdivision of wave C in a zigzag correction.

• Ending diagonals are typically characterized by having overlapping wave 1 and 4, and they often form a wedge shape. However, it's important to note that the overlap between wave 1 and 4 is not a strict condition; it may or may not happen.

• The subdivision of an ending diagonal can follow either a 3-3-3-3-3 or a 5-3-5-3-5 pattern.

By understanding the features of ending diagonals, traders and analysts can better identify and interpret this unique wave pattern within the Elliott Wave structure, aiding in more accurate analysis and forecasting in the financial markets.

3.5 Motive Sequence

Motive waves traditionally move in the same direction as the primary trend, but in today's context, we believe they don't necessarily have to be limited to impulses. Instead, we prefer to refer to it as a motive sequence. A motive sequence is simply an incomplete sequence of waves or swings. While the structure of the waves can be corrective, analyzing the sequence of swings helps us determine whether the move is complete or if we should expect an extension in the current direction.

The concept of a motive sequence is akin to the Fibonacci number sequence. If we observe the number of swings on the chart aligning with one of the numbers in the motive sequence (e.g., 5, 9, 13, 17, 21, 25, 29, ...), we can anticipate the current trend to extend further.

By recognizing and applying the motive sequence concept, traders and analysts can gain insights into potential trend extensions, enhancing their ability to forecast market movements with greater accuracy.

4) Waves Personality

4.1 Wave 1 and wave 2

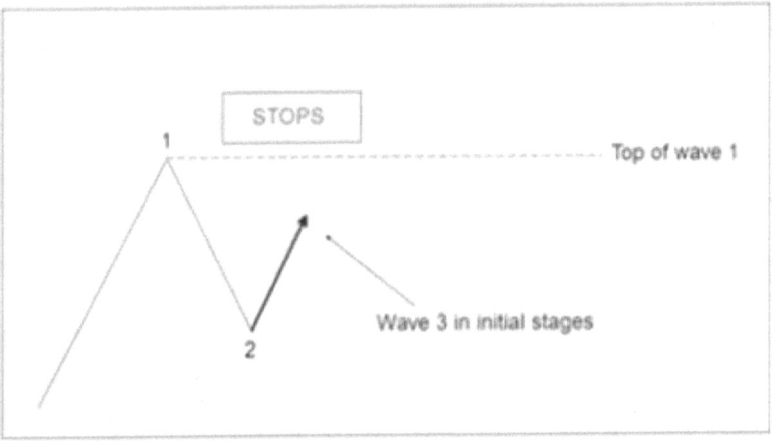

Wave 1: In Elliott Wave Theory, wave one is often not immediately apparent when it begins. At the start of a new bull market, the fundamental news is predominantly negative. The previous trend is considered to still hold strong. Fundamental analysts continue to revise their earnings estimates downward, and the overall economic outlook may not appear robust. Sentiment surveys show a bearish sentiment prevailing, and put options are in high demand, resulting in elevated implied volatility in the options market. While volume might increase slightly as prices rise, it may not be significant enough to catch the attention of many technical analysts.

Wave 2: In Elliott Wave Theory, wave two serves as a correction to wave one, but it must not extend beyond the starting point of wave one. During this phase, the negative news may persist. As prices retest the previous low, bearish sentiment builds rapidly, and pessimistic voices emphasize that the bear market is still firmly established. However, positive signs start to emerge for those who observe carefully: volume should be lower during wave two compared to wave one, prices typically do not retrace more than 61.8% (as explained in the Fibonacci section below) of the gains made in wave one, and the price decline should follow a three-wave pattern.

By understanding the characteristics of wave one and wave two in the Elliott Wave Theory, traders and analysts can better identify and interpret these crucial stages of market movements, aiding them in making well-informed trading decisions.

4.2 Wave 3

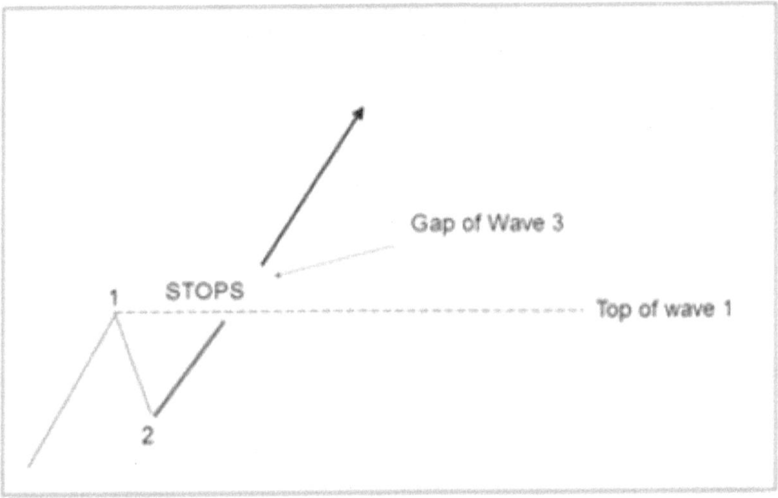

Wave 3: In Elliott Wave Theory, wave three is typically the largest and most powerful wave within a trend (although some research suggests that in commodity markets, wave five could be the largest). Positive news prevails during this phase, and fundamental analysts start to raise their earnings estimates. Prices surge rapidly, and any corrections that occur are brief and shallow. Those looking to enter the market on a pullback may find themselves missing out, as wave three gains momentum quickly.

At the beginning of wave three, the news might still lean towards bearish, and most market participants remain negative. However, as wave three reaches its midpoint, "the crowd" often shifts to a more bullish stance, joining the new uptrend. Wave three often extends wave one by a ratio of 1.618:1.

During the wave three rally, the price surpasses the top of wave one. This breakthrough triggers stop-loss orders, resulting in gaps in the price movement. Gaps can be a strong indication of an ongoing wave three. As the stops are taken out, the wave three rally captures the attention of traders and market participants.

Understanding the dynamics of wave three is crucial for traders and analysts as it represents a significant and highly profitable phase within the Elliott Wave Theory, providing valuable insights for successful trading strategies.

4.3 Wave 4

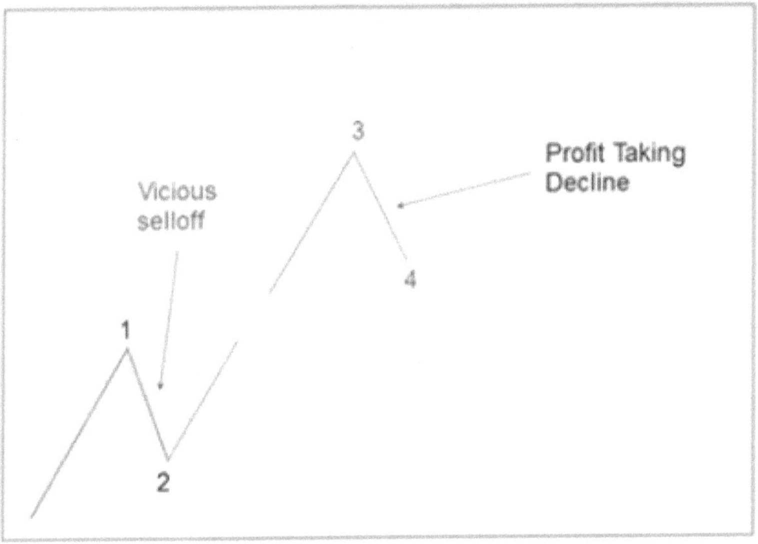

Towards the conclusion of wave 4, increased buying activity emerges, leading to a renewed rally in prices. Wave four is typically recognized as a clear corrective phase. During this period, prices may move sideways for an extended duration, and the retracement of wave four usually remains below 38.2% of the magnitude of wave three. Volume during wave four is notably lower than that observed during wave three.

This phase presents a favorable opportunity to buy on a pullback, particularly if one comprehends the potential prospects for wave 5. Nevertheless, fourth waves can be frustrating for traders due to their limited progress within the broader trend.

Being able to identify and interpret wave four correctly is essential for traders, as it allows them to make informed decisions about market entry points and potential price movements during the upcoming wave five, maximizing their trading opportunities.

4.4 Wave 5

In Elliott Wave Theory, wave five represents the final phase of the dominant trend. During this stage, the news becomes overwhelmingly positive, and a bullish sentiment prevails among market participants. However, it is at this point that many average investors tend to buy in, often just before the market reaches its peak. Volume in wave five is typically lower than in wave three, and several momentum indicators may start showing divergences, where prices reach new highs, but the indicators fail to reach new peaks.

As a major bull market comes to an end, the bears may be subject to ridicule, as previous forecasts for a market top might have been dismissed. Despite reaching a new high above the top of wave three, the enthusiasm and strength seen in the wave three rally are often lacking in wave five. The advance in wave five is driven by a small group of traders, and the rate of power or strength within the wave five advance is comparatively small when compared to the wave three advance.

Recognizing the characteristics of wave five is vital for traders and investors to avoid falling into common behavioral traps and to make well-informed decisions during this critical phase of the market cycle.

4.5 Wave A, B, and C

Wave A: Corrections are typically harder to identify than impulse moves. In wave A of a bear market, the fundamental news is usually still positive. Most analysts see the drop as a correction in a still-active bull market. Some technical indicators that accompany wave A include increased volume, rising implied volatility in the options markets, and possibly a turn higher in open interest in related futures markets.

Wave B: Prices reverse higher, which many see as a resumption of the now long-gone bull market. Those familiar with classical technical analysis may see the peak as the right shoulder of a head and shoulders reversal pattern. The volume during wave B should be lower than in wave A. By this point, fundamentals are probably no longer improving, but they most likely have not yet turned negative.

Wave C: Prices move impulsively lower in five waves. Volume picks up, and by the third leg of wave C, almost everyone realizes that a bear market is firmly entrenched. Wave C is typically at least as large as wave A and often extends to 1.618 times wave A or beyond.

5) Corrective Waves

The classic definition of corrective waves is waves that move against the trend of one greater degree. Corrective waves have a lot more variety and are less clearly identifiable compared to impulse waves. Sometimes it can be rather difficult to identify corrective patterns until they are completed. However, as we have explained above, both trend and counter-trend can unfold in a corrective pattern in today's market, especially in the forex market. Corrective waves are probably better defined as waves that move in three, but never in five. Only motive waves are fives.

There are five types of corrective patterns:

- Zigzag (5-3-5)
- Flat (3-3-5)
- Triangle (3-3-3-3-3)
- Double three: A combination of two corrective patterns above
- Triple three: A combination of three corrective patterns above.

5.1 Zigzag

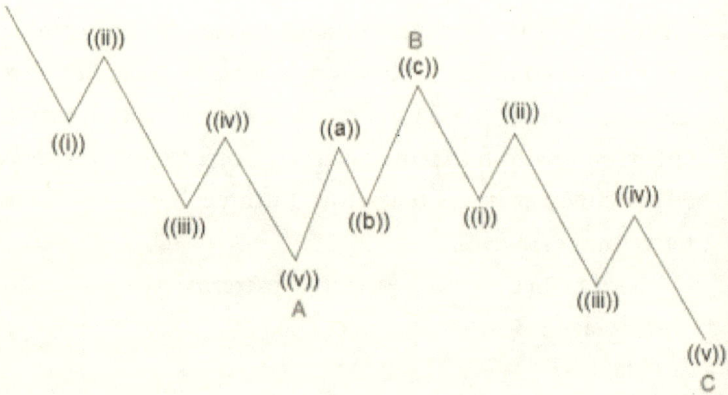

Guidelines for Zigzag :

- Zigzag is a corrective 3-wave structure labelled as ABC.
- Subdivision of wave A and C is 5 waves, either impulse or diagonal.
- Wave B can be any corrective structure.
- Zigzag is a 5-3-5 structure.

Fibonacci Ratio Relationship:

- Wave B = 50%, 61.8%, 76.4%, or 85.4% of wave A.
- Wave C = 61.8%, 100%, or 123.6% of wave A.

- If wave C = 161.8% of wave A, wave C can be a wave 3 of a 5-wave impulse. Thus, one way to label between ABC and impulse is whether the third swing has an extension or not.

5.2 Flat

A flat correction is a 3-wave corrective move labelled as ABC. Although the labelling is the same, flat differs from zigzag in the subdivision of wave A. Whereas Zigzag is a 5-3-5 structure, Flat is a 3-3-5 structure. There are three different types of Flats: Regular, Irregular/Expanded, and Running Flats.

5.2.1 Regular Flats

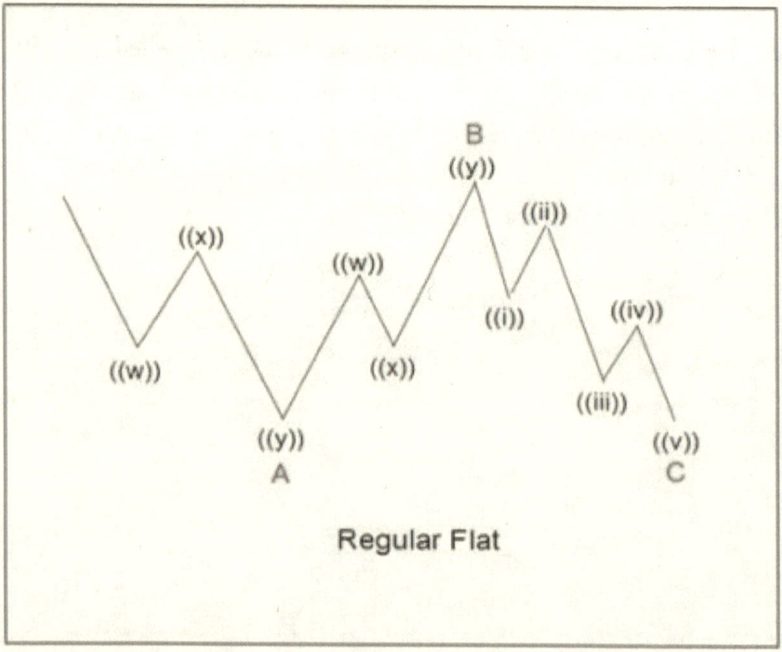

Guidelines for Regular Flats:

- A corrective 3-wave move labelled as ABC.
- Subdivision of wave A and B is in 3 waves.
- Subdivision of wave C is in 5 waves (impulse/diagonal).
- Subdivision of wave A and B can be in any corrective 3-wave structure, including zigzag, flat, double three, and triple three.
- Wave B terminates near the start of wave A.
- Wave C generally terminates slightly beyond the end of wave A.
- Wave C needs to have momentum divergence.

Fibonacci Ratio Relationship:

- Wave B = 90% of wave A.

- Wave C = 61.8%, 100%, or 123.6% of wave AB.

5.2.2 Expanded Flats

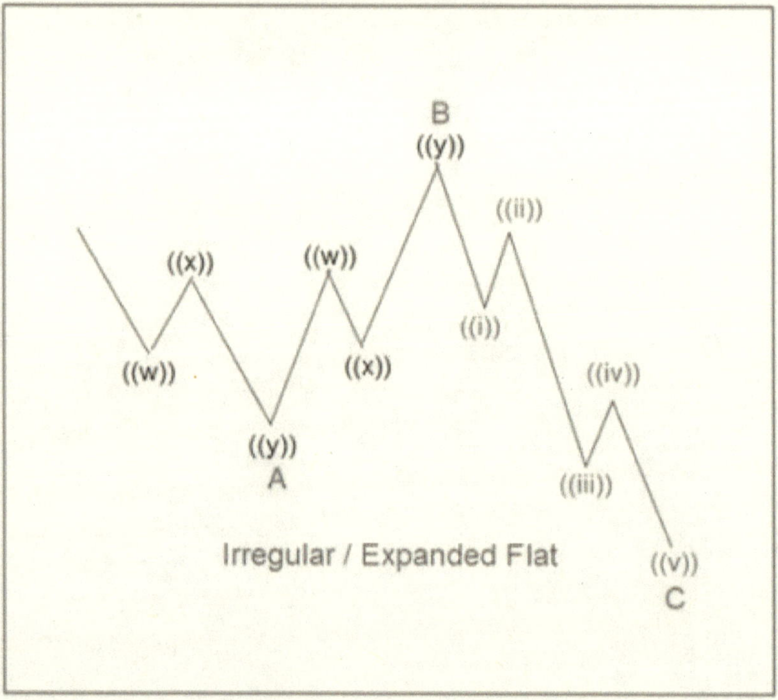

Guidelines for Expanded Flats:

- A corrective 3-wave move labelled as ABC.
- Subdivision of wave A and B is in 3 waves.
- Subdivision of wave C is in 5 waves (impulse/diagonal).
- Subdivision of wave A and B can be in any corrective 3-wave structure, including zigzag, flat, double three, and triple three.
- Wave B of the 3-3-5 pattern terminates beyond the starting level of wave A.
- Wave C ends substantially beyond the ending level of wave A.
- Wave C needs to have momentum divergence.

Fibonacci Ratio Relationship:
- Wave B = 123.6% of wave A.

- Wave C = 123.6% – 161.8% of wave AB.

5.2.3 Running Flats

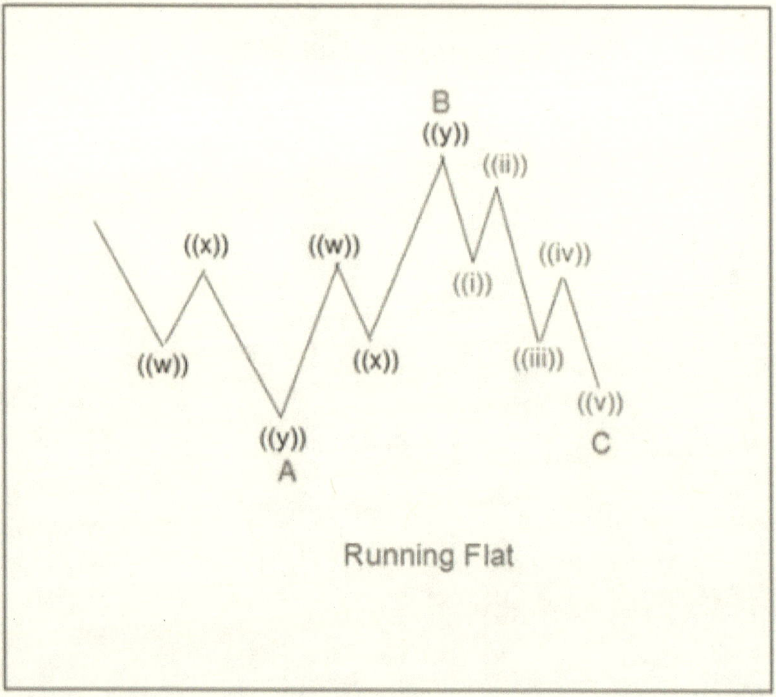

Guidelines for Running Flat:

- A corrective 3-wave move labelled as ABC.
- Subdivision of wave A and B is in 3 waves.
- Subdivision of wave C is in 5 waves (impulse/diagonal).
- Subdivision of wave A and B can be in any corrective 3-wave structure, including zigzag, flat, double three, and triple three.
- Wave B of the 3-3-5 pattern terminates substantially beyond the starting level of wave A as in an expanded flat.
- Wave C fails to travel the full distance, falling short of the level where wave A ended.

- Wave C needs to have momentum divergence.

Fibonacci Ratio Relationship:

- Wave B = 123.6% of wave A.

- Wave C = 61.8% – 100% of wave AB.

5.3 Triangles

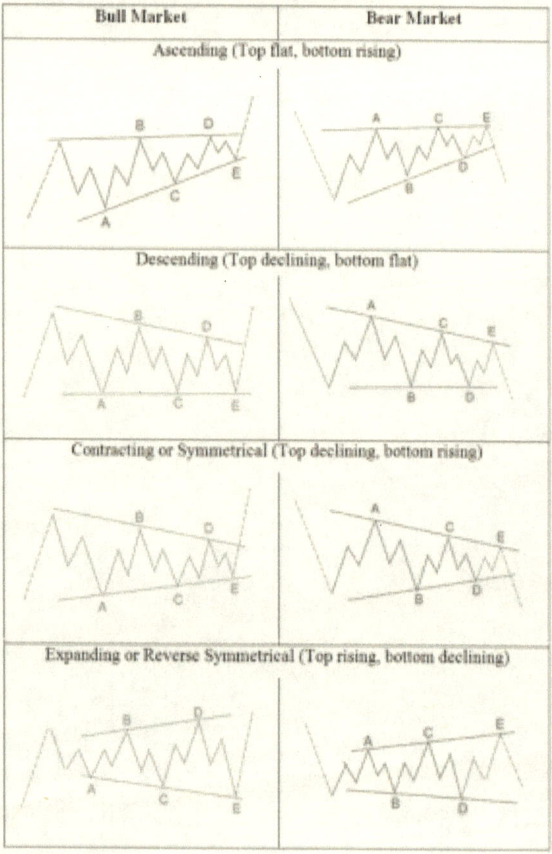

Guidelines for Triangles:

- Corrective structure labelled as ABCDE.
- Usually happens in wave B or wave 4.
- Subdivided into five waves with 3-3-3-3-3 pattern.
- RSI (Relative Strength Index) also needs to support the triangle in every time frame.

- Subdivision of ABCDE can be either abc, wxy, or flat.

5.4 Double Three

Double three is a sideways combination of two corrective patterns. It is labelled as WXY and consists of seven swings. Wave W and wave Y subdivisions can be zigzag, flat, double three of smaller degree, or triple three of smaller degree. Wave X can be any corrective structure. In terms of Fibonacci ratios, wave X is typically 50%, 61.8%, 76.4%, or 85.4% of wave W, while wave Y is usually 61.8%, 100%, or 123.6% of wave W. Wave Y should not exceed 161.8% of wave W. Below are examples of different combinations of two corrective structures which form the double threes.

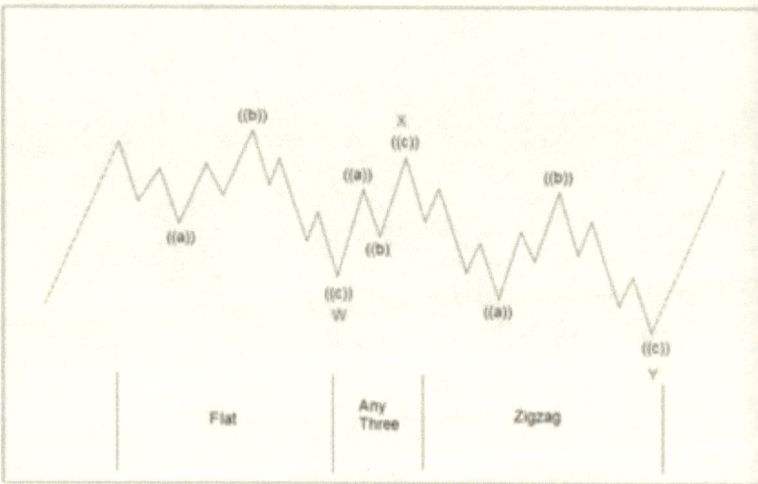

Above figure is a combination of a flat and a zigzag

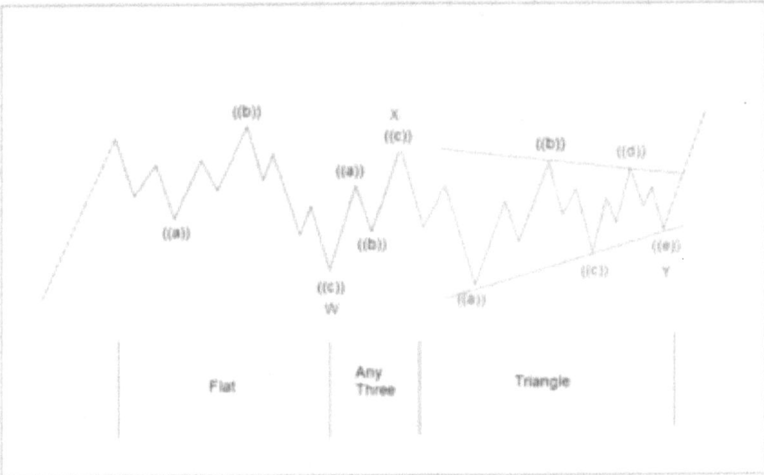

Above figure is a combination of a flat and a triangle

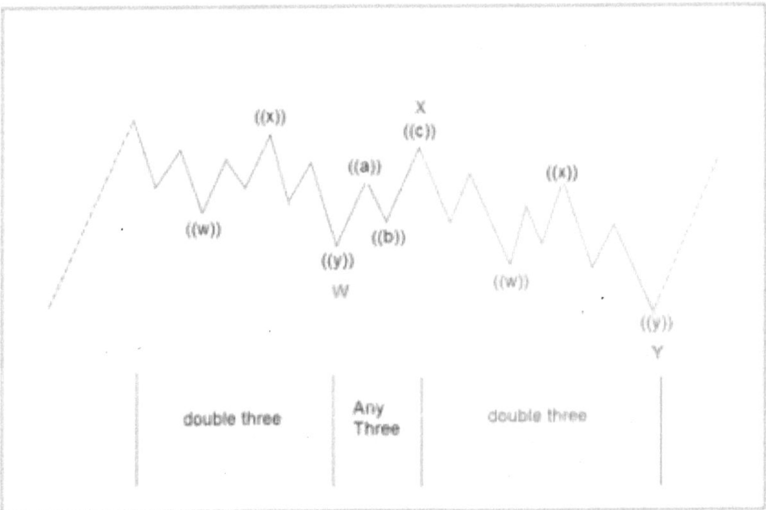

Above figure is a combination of two double threes of lesser degree

5.5 Triple Three

Triple three is a sideways combination of three corrective patterns in Elliott Wave Theory. It is labelled as WXYXZ and consists of eleven swings. Wave W, wave Y, and wave Z subdivisions can be zigzag, flat, double three of smaller degree, or triple three of smaller degree. Wave X can be any corrective structure. In terms of Fibonacci ratios, wave X is typically 50%, 61.8%, 76.4%, or 85.4% of wave W, while wave Z is usually 61.8%, 100%, or 123.6% of wave W. Wave Y should not exceed 161.8% of wave W, as it could potentially become an impulsive wave 3. Below are examples of different combinations of three corrective structures which form the triple threes.

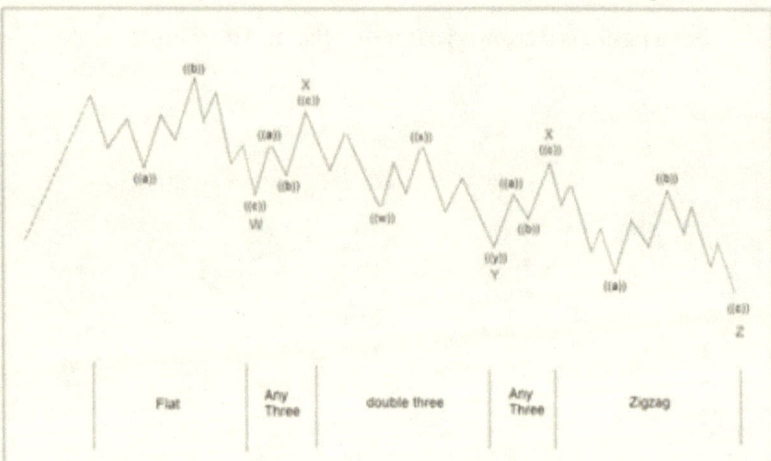

Above figure is a combination of a flat, double three, and zigzag.

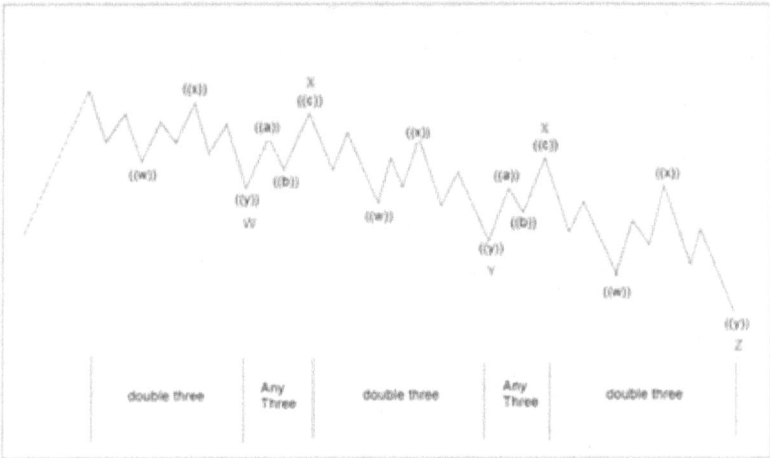

Above figure is a combination of three double threes

Refernces

1. "Elliott Wave Principle: Key to Market Behavior" par Robert R. Prechter Jr. et A.J. Frost

2. "Mastering Elliott Wave Principle: Elementary Concepts, Wave Patterns, and Practice Exercises" par Constance Brown

3. "Elliott Wave Principle and Theory" par Ralph Nelson Elliott

4. "Five Waves to Financial Freedom: Learn Elliott Wave Analysis" par Ramki N. Ramakrishnan

5. "Elliott Wave Principle: A Key to Market Behavior" par Robert R. Prechter Jr. et A.J. Frost

6. "Elliott Wave Principle Applied to the Foreign Exchange Markets" par Robert Balan

7. "The Elliott Wave Writings of A.J. Frost and Richard Russell" par A.J. Frost et Richard Russell

8. "How to Trade Elliott Wave with Fibonacci" par Robert Fischer

9. "Applying Elliott Wave Theory Profitably" par Steven W. Poser

10. "The Visual Guide to Elliott Wave Trading" par Wayne Gorman et Jeffrey Kennedy

Don't miss out!

Visit the website below and you can sign up to receive emails whenever Khalid Madih publishes a new book. There's no charge and no obligation.

https://books2read.com/r/B-A-RUWZ-FWPMC

Also by Khalid Madih

Elliote Wave Theory

About the Author

Khalid Madih Trader with 5 years experience across multiple markets. Skilled in chart pattern recognition and Elliott Wave analysis. Successfully trades stocks, forex, commodities, and crypto assets. Passionate about honing trading skills. Runs a YouTube channel teaching Wave Theory strategies.

www.ingramcontent.com/pod-product-compliance
Lightning Source LLC
LaVergne TN
LVHW090431210926
848480LV00002B/778